# STUDS & SPIKES

30

CREATIVE PROJECTS

FOR CUSTOMIZED

FASHION

## KIRSTEN NUNEZ

Laurence King Publishing

**LAURENCE KING**

Published in 2014
by Laurence King Publishing Ltd
361–373 City Road
London EC1V 1LR
tel +44 20 7841 6900
fax +44 20 7841 6910
e-mail enquiries@laurenceking.com
www.laurenceking.com

Design © 2014 Laurence King Publishing
Text and photography © 2014 Kirsten Nunez

A catalogue record for this book is
available from the British Library.

ISBN 978 178067 369 1

Designed by Evelin Kasikov

Printed in China

To everyone
who just wants to do
what they love.

**8** Introduction

**10** DIY Basics

**14** Tips and Tricks

**16** Ideas for Inspiration

**18** CLOTHING

**58** ACCESSORIES

**98** JEWELRY

**138** SHOES

**20** No-Sew Scarf Vest/ Waistcoat

**24** Stamped Leggings

**28** Contrast-Trim Blazer

**32** Party Skirt

**36** Scarf-Panel Denim Vest/ Waistcoat

**40** Faux-Studded Leather Jacket

**46** Fabric-Corner Shorts

**50** Gathered Dress

**54** Watercolor Jeans

**60** Sunglass-Case Clutch

**64** Elastic Brad Belt

**68** Stone-Strap Watch

**72** Glitter Sunglasses

**76** Abstract Tote Bag

**80** Sweater Circle Scarf

**84** Knotted Headband

**88** Painted Floral Clutch

**94** Embellished Beanie

**100** Vinyl Tube Bracelet

**104** Triangle Drop Earrings

**108** Statement Ring

**112** Fabric-Wrapped Bangle

**116** Leather Charm Earrings

**120** Hardware Bracelet

**126** Beaded Circle Necklace

**132** Chain-and-Thread Bracelet

**140** Studded-Sole Shoes

**144** Color-Blocked Pumps

**148** Floral Heels

**152** Ribbon-Bow Flats

**156** Sources

**157** Glossary

**158** Acknowledgments

**159** About the Author

**160** Index of Projects by Difficulty Level

# Introduction

Like many other crafters and designers, my love for creating showed at a very young age. I remember being fascinated with the idea of making something from nothing. From my lunch box to my notebook, I decorated everything I owned. I often borrowed craft books from the library, only to borrow them again in the hope of mastering the projects they held. I painted, I drew, I took things apart and put them back together. I taught myself how to sew in high school, then started a jewelry business out of my college dorm room. By the time I started graduate school, I had realized that handmade fashion was the undoubtedly the best form of self-expression. Of course, fashion itself can provide that … but the do-it-yourself (DIY) aspect presents an unrivaled opportunity for personalization. My mind was constantly overflowing with ideas, which left me with a need to share my projects. I decided to do this in the form of a blog, which would allow me to interact with readers. In 2010, Studs & Pearls was born.

This book embodies the main concept of Studs & Pearls: taking ordinary craft, fashion and hardware supplies and using them in interesting ways. However, this is far from your average DIY fashion book. Aside from the 30 tutorials, each project is followed by several different versions, which I call "Inspirations." Each Inspiration is similar to the original project, but differs in material or technique. After all, it only takes one small change to completely alter the style and vibe of a finished product.

In total—tutorials and Inspirations combined—there are more than 130 projects in this book. The tutorials serve as guides, just to get you started. At the same time, the Inspirations are simply ideas. They show that we're not limited to what's in front of us, whether it's the steps in the tutorial or the mass produced items in a store. There are no boundaries to the creative thought process, and there are certainly no rules.

In my eyes, DIY fashion is about more than just recreating something that walks down the runway or is featured in a magazine. Of course, both of these things can spark some inspiration. But it doesn't have to stop there. DIY fashion displays a combination of crafting and style, enabling us to create something completely unique. It looks past the monetary value of fashion and focuses on the creator's self-expression. There is nothing out there that can represent who you are any better than something you have made. I encourage you to add a personal touch to every project in this book; take it, run with it, and make it your own.

xo,
Kirsten

# DIY BASICS

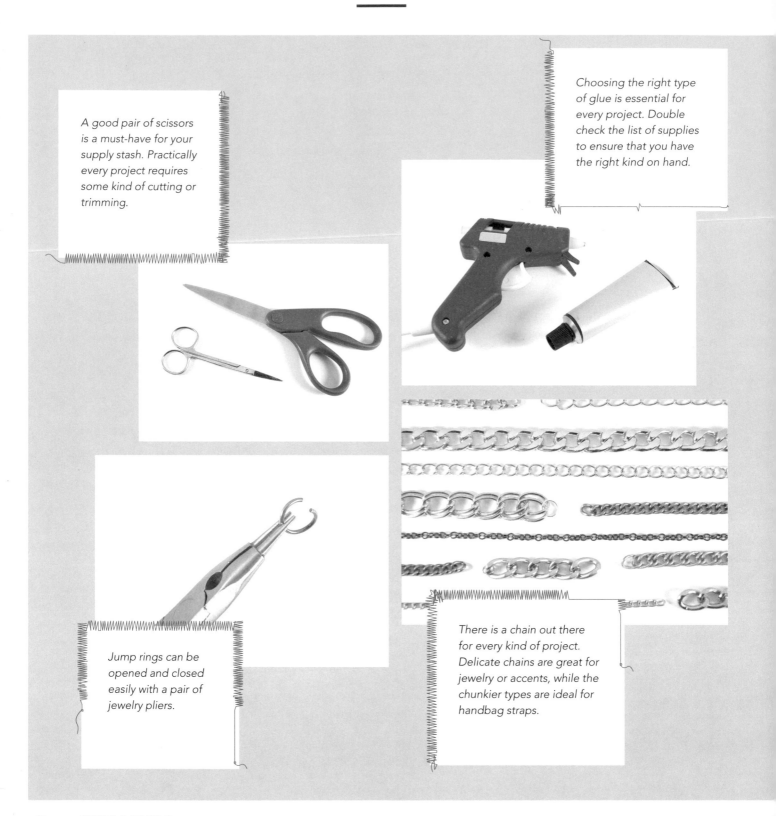

A good pair of scissors is a must-have for your supply stash. Practically every project requires some kind of cutting or trimming.

Choosing the right type of glue is essential for every project. Double check the list of supplies to ensure that you have the right kind on hand.

Jump rings can be opened and closed easily with a pair of jewelry pliers.

There is a chain out there for every kind of project. Delicate chains are great for jewelry or accents, while the chunkier types are ideal for handbag straps.

# DIY BASICS

## FABRIC

Whether you're using a couple scraps or an entire yard, *fabric* is often the core of many fashion projects. Old clothing is a really great (and inexpensive) source for materials such as cotton, silk, and denim.

## SCISSORS

Two essential pairs to have on hand are *multi-purpose* and *fabric scissors*. Multi-purpose scissors are used to cut a variety of materials, such as string or cardboard. Fabric scissors or dressmakers' shears are designed solely for fabric material: to avoid blunting them, use them only for fabric.

## MEASURING TOOLS

*Rulers* and *measuring tapes* are necessary for almost every project. Aside from helping you measure accurate lengths and widths, a handheld ruler is useful for creating straight edges. Measuring tapes are much more flexible, allowing you to measure curved objects, such as your wrist.

## GLUE

For DIY fashion, the types of glue that you will often use include *hot glue*, *fabric glue*, and *strong craft glue*. Hot glue is a fast-drying adhesive that can join a variety of surfaces together. Caution should be used, as the temperature of the glue can increase quite fast. Fabric glue can be used to adhere two fabrics, as well as attaching ribbon or trimming to fabric. After 24 hours, fabric glue dries clear and flexible. Garments can then be washed as they normally would. Strong craft glue is considered to be industrial strength, and forms an extremely strong bond between two surfaces. This is excellent for jewelry components and heavier materials such as metal or leather. Don't forget to use this type of glue in a well-ventilated area.

## WRITING UTENSILS

A simple #2/HB *pencil* or a *pen* can used to mark measurements and create patterns. *Tailor's chalk* works perfectly for clothing and darker surfaces. Light rubbing will easily wipe away the chalk.

## BRUSHES

A *soft-bristled art brush* can be used to apply paint to different surfaces. A brush designed for all mediums is appropriate for the projects in this book. Thin brushes are good for smaller areas and finer lines. *Foam brushes* are inexpensive and can be purchased in assorted widths and sizes.

## PLIERS

Many *jewelry pliers* are "3-in-1," featuring rounded tips, a flat portion known as the needle nose, and a wire cutter. The round tips can create wire loops, as well as bending and grasping components. The center part is useful for flattening or holding pieces. The cutting tool can trim thin chain, wire, or cord. *Hardware pliers* are great for taking apart heavy chains or even accessories such as belts or handbags.

## WIRE CUTTERS

As an alternative to 3-in-1 pliers, *wire cutters* can be used to cut different gauges of wire. They are also ideal for cutting stems off faux flowers.

## BUTTON SHANK REMOVER

A button that has a loop on the back is known as a shank button. This type of button can be sewn onto fabric with needle and thread. A *button shank remover*, which can be found in the button section of craft stores, is designed to remove the loop. This creates a flat surface, allowing the button to be used as an embellishment. This tool can be used on acrylic plastic buttons.

## CHAINS

Often used in jewelry making, *chains* are available in an endless variety of styles, thicknesses, and metal finishes. Chains can be trimmed by separating the links with pliers or wire cutters. The type of chain you choose will significantly contribute to the overall look and feel of your finished project. Curb chains are made from slightly curved oval links, rolo chains consist of round metal components, and cable chains involve flat circles or ovals. These are just a few of the basic types of chain you are likely to find at the craft store.

# DIY BASICS

## JEWELRY FINDINGS

Like chains, jewelry findings can be found in different finishes, such as gold, silver, and brass. The most commonly used findings are *jump rings* and *clasps*. Jump rings are metal hoops that are used to join metal components together; they can be opened and closed with a pair of pliers, and are available in different sizes and gauges. *Clasps* are connected to chain using a jump ring. When the clasp is opened, it can attach to another jump ring. This will keep a bracelet or necklace in place while it is worn. Spring rings are circular shaped, while lobster clasps resemble a teardrop.

*Ring blanks* are another type of finding that is often used in DIY fashion. These metal rings are adjustable and have a flat "blank" surface onto which materials can be glued. *Earring hooks* are curved pieces of metal with a small loop that can be opened and closed with pliers. Components hang off on this loop, creating an earring. Rubber backings can be used to keep earring hooks in place while worn.

## EMBELLISHMENTS

An *embellishment* is used to decorate an item. These can include practically anything, such as buttons, stones, sequins, gems, and appliqués. Vintage brooches or broken jewelry can also make interesting embellishments. Use your imagination!

## TRIMMINGS AND RIBBON

*Trimmings*, or trims, are strands of material used as an ornament or decoration. Trimmings are often made out of lace, sequins, or fringe. *Ribbons* are thin strips of fabric that fall into the category of trims. They can be found in materials such as leather, silk, or velvet. Trimmings and ribbon are often sold by the yard or meter.

## SEAM RIPPER/UNPICKER

This tool might well be considered a crafter's best friend. A *seam ripper*, or *unpicker*, has a handle and a sharp, curved metal end, which is used to take apart stitches. It is so much easier than using a pair of scissors, and will save you a lot of time.

## PINS

*Pins* are extremely useful for holding fabrics and hems in place before sewing them. You only have so many hands, after all. It is especially helpful to pin a garment when you are trying to find the right fit before actually sewing it. Pins can be stored on a pincushion or even a scrap piece of fabric.

## NEEDLE AND THREAD

A simple hand *needle* for hand-sewing is a must-have for any DIY crafter. Whether you're stitching up a hole or adding embellishments, needles can really come in handy. *All-purpose thread* will work perfectly fine for most tutorials. As you work on more projects over time, you can always purchase different thread in the colors that you need.

## IRON

If you're working with fabric, it's a good idea to use an *iron* to eliminate any wrinkles. Your finished project will have a greater chance of looking pristine and well put together. Don't forget to iron the fabric or garment inside out, as well. Check clothing tags for specific ironing instructions, and be sure to choose the right fabric setting on your iron. A sturdy, flat surface such as an ironing board is the most appopriate surface to work on.

## SEWING MACHINE

Last but not least … a *sewing machine*. It must be stressed that while owning one is certainly useful, it is NOT a necessity. With patience and perseverance, hand-sewing can definitely take the place of machine sewing for the projects in this book. However, don't be afraid to try and learn how to use one. Knowing how to stitch just a basic straight line can open up so many possibilities.

# DIY BASICS

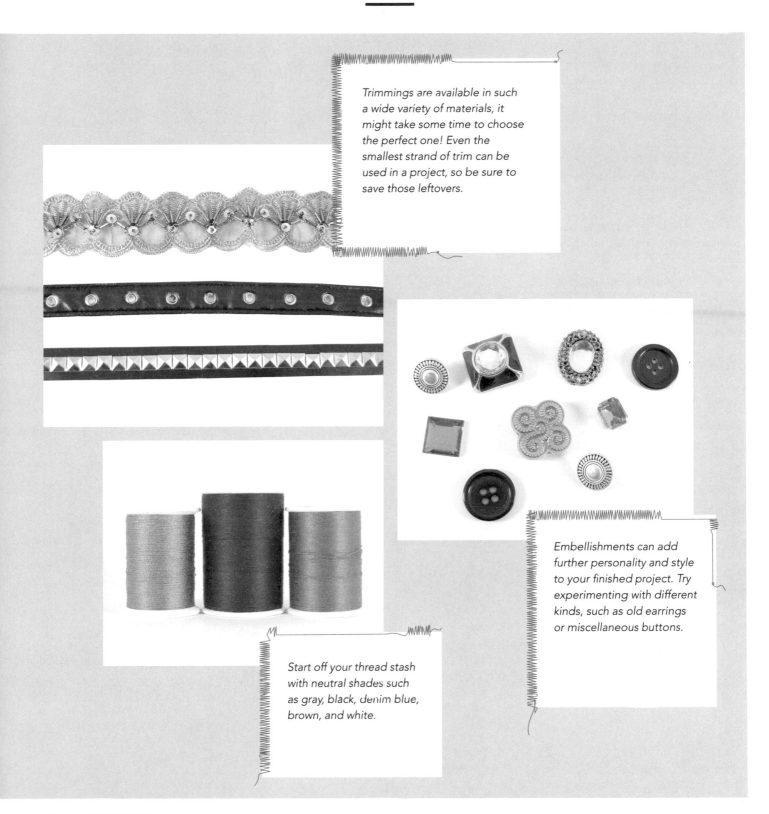

Trimmings are available in such a wide variety of materials, it might take some time to choose the perfect one! Even the smallest strand of trim can be used in a project, so be sure to save those leftovers.

Embellishments can add further personality and style to your finished project. Try experimenting with different kinds, such as old earrings or miscellaneous buttons.

Start off your thread stash with neutral shades such as gray, black, denim blue, brown, and white.

# TIPS AND TRICKS

### Re-Purpose

Supplies don't always have to come straight from the store. Your wardrobe and collection of supplies may be home to many potential materials. For example, jeans can be cut into shorts, while practically any garment can be cut apart for its fabric.

### Do Some Research

Understand your basic supplies and what they are used for. Thanks to the Internet, diagrams and videos are just a few clicks away. Search engines are great for scoping out methods that you might not be familiar with.

## TIPS

### Write a Shopping List

Purchasing supplies will be easier if you have a list on hand. It might even help to photocopy the tutorial to refer to while shopping. This is exceptionally useful when a project calls for materials in specific measurements or types.

### Ask Questions

If you have a question, don't hesitate to ask an employee for guidance. Not only will they be able to help you find the right product, but they can also answer any questions regarding special discounts or possible alternatives.

### Shop Secondhand

Thrift store items can offer both inexpensive and eccentric materials to work with. The number one rule to successful thrifting? *Be picky.* Don't settle for something just because the price tag caught your eye. Purchase something only when it's really what you're looking for, and you'll get the most out of your spending.

### Overbuy

It's always wise to buy a bit more than you actually need. Mistakes happen, and overbuying will allow you to continue your project without another shopping trip. You also never know when the necessary supplies will go out of stock … so *always* overbuy. Any leftovers can always be saved for future creations, and might even spark some new ideas.

### Find a Work Space

Clear out your desk or dining table when working on a project. Making projects in a cluttered area can be extremely distracting. You'll also spend a lot less time rummaging through items to find what you need.

### Organize

As most crafters and designers know, a collection of supplies can be overwhelming. Try assigning a designated spot for each type of material. Tackle boxes are appropriate for odds and ends, and baskets are great for bulkier items. When it comes to fabric, store large remnants on hangers and fold smaller pieces into boxes. A shelf is best for bottles of glue and paint. When you can actually see what you have, creating will be so much easier.

# TIPS AND TRICKS

## Test It Out

If you're wary about taking on a project, give it a shot with spare supplies before making the "real thing." This is especially useful if you're planning to work with a favorite item that can't be replaced. You'll also gain the experience and confidence to carry out the project.

## Overestimate

This tip accompanies the concept of overbuying. When cutting materials such as string or fabric, start with more than what is indicated in the tutorial. Remember: you can always take some away, but you can't add it back.

## Take Your Time

Read the entire tutorial before starting. This will give you an idea of how the project will eventually come together, and how each step relates to the next one.

## Have Fun

The most important tip of all: enjoy! Don't be too hard on yourself if you make a mistake and have to start over—this is exactly how you'll learn. DIY isn't about making the "perfect" project … it's about pushing your imagination and making something that's all you.

## TRICKS

- If you don't have liquid seam sealant on hand, clear nail polish can keep raw edges from fraying.

- Stick a magnetic strip onto your sewing machine for a quick and easy holder for pins.

- A strip of fabric tied around a pair of fabric scissors will remind you of its intended purpose.

- For a foolproof storage solution, wrap ribbons and trims around cardboard. If you'd like, cover the cardboard with adhesive paper. Secure the trims with a piece of tape, and store them in a drawer or box. Tangled strands of ribbon will then be a thing of the past.

- Use a lint roller to quickly clean up those pesky bits of thread and fabric.

- Long strips of masking tape can serve as a guide for cutting fabric in a straight line, as seen in the *No-Sew Scarf Vest/Waistcoat* project (page 20).

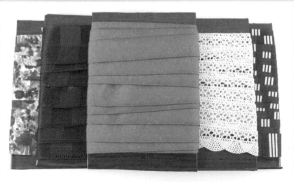

# IDEAS FOR INSPIRATION

### TAKE NOTE

The moment an idea comes to you, write it down. Keeping a small notebook in your bag or on your desk can help encourage your creative thought process. You might not know where to take the idea at that very second—but give it some time, and you might be able to build it upon it later.

### SNAP A PICTURE

Technology has granted us the ability to take photos any time and anywhere. Take photos of whatever you find to be inspiring, whether it is the scenery or a fashion item. By documenting inspiration in a visual form, you'll give potential ideas a chance to flourish.

### GIVE IT A BREAK

When you're stuck on the next step to take, there is nothing wrong with taking a breather. Time away will clear your mind, letting you come back with a different approach. You might even unexpectedly stumble across inspiration.

# IDEAS FOR INSPIRATION

### SHOP YOUR CLOSET

Before heading to the store, browse what you already own. Clothing that you rarely wear holds a lot of potential. Every now and then, take a look at your closet and see what can add or alter. You never know what you might come up with, especially as you accumulate materials and ideas over time.

### EXPLORE

There is so much inspiration around us. Don't be afraid to explore new things: Pick up a magazine you've never heard of, visit that store you always walked by, buy some materials you've never worked with. Look beyond what is readily available, and you'll be surprised at the new things you'll learn.

### CREATE AN INSPIRATION BOARD

Fill up a board with photos and items that catch your attention. These can include anything from magazine cut-outs to fabric scraps. Eventually, you'll get a sense of your personal taste and style. To make an inexpensive inspiration board, take an old large frame. Remove the glass and replace with a sheet of cork trimmed to fit the frame's dimensions. Insert the original cardboard backing, and you have an instant inspiration board. Hang up inspiring items with double-sided tape or pins.

# CLOTHING

In the world of DIY, clothing tends to have an intimidating reputation. However, the best projects are often the most basic. Different types of ribbon can bring in texture, while embellishments can add some sparkle. Sometimes it's all about *how* you cut something, as seen in the No-Sew Scarf Vest/Waistcoat (page 20). A few simple hand stitches can completely transform a garment with anything from fabric scraps to trims. And if you do know how to use a sewing machine? You don't have to be a Project Runway contestant to create an outstanding piece. You'll be surprised at what you can do with just a straight stitch.

Before starting a clothing project, take a look at your own closet. Look for garments that you barely wear or could use that extra something. By "shopping" your own wardrobe, you can make the most of what you own at the same time as emphasizing your personal style.

# No-Sew Scarf Vest/Waistcoat

The most innovative ideas are also often the simplest. With a few strategically placed cuts, a scarf can easily double as a draped vest/waistcoat. If you've just begun to take on DIY projects, this 2-in-1 garment is a great starting point.

Difficulty Level

## SUPPLIES

---

**Large Square Scarf**
**Fabric Scissors**
**Masking Tape**
**Ruler**
**Liquid Seam Sealant**

---

**1** Find the center line of the scarf. About 3½ in (9 cm) on either side of the center fold, and 5 in (13 cm) from the top, place a diagonal strip of masking tape 13 in (33 cm) long.

**2** Cut the scarf along the tape.

**3** Remove the tape and apply liquid seam sealant along the raw edges.

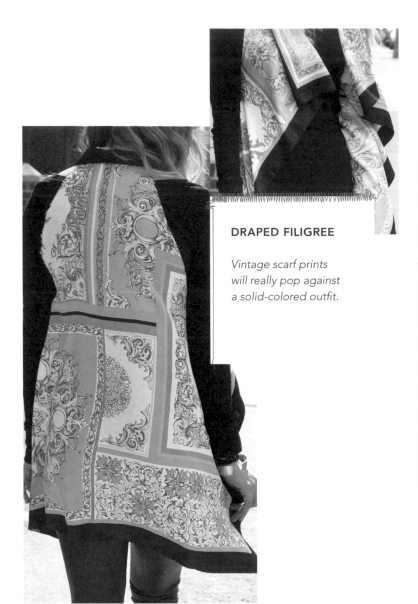

**FOR INFINITE POSSIBILITIES, SUBSTITUTE THE SCARF WITH A SEGMENT OF FABRIC MEASURING AT LEAST 30 X 30 IN (75 X 75 CM)**

### DRAPED FILIGREE

*Vintage scarf prints will really pop against a solid-colored outfit.*

### CASUALLY IN-VESTED

*A vest/waistcoat made from jersey can take your little black dress from night to day.*

## DRAPED IN LACE

*Lace makes for a breezy, lightweight garment.*

# Stamped Leggings

When it comes to creating prints and patterns, you don't have to be a screenprinting pro to create you very own. Thick craft foam, usually found in the kids' section of craft stores, can be used to make a simple stamp. Just one sheet of this budget-friendly material is enough for many different stamps.

## BEFORE YOU START

Run a lint roller or some masking tape over the leggings. This will give you a clean slate to work with, ensuring that any lint doesn't find its way into the fabric paint.

## SUPPLIES

---

Leggings
Paintbrush
Fabric Paint
Scissors
Wooden Spool
Craft Foam
Strong Craft Glue

---

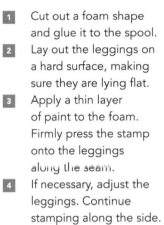

1. Cut out a foam shape and glue it to the spool.
2. Lay out the leggings on a hard surface, making sure they are lying flat.
3. Apply a thin layer of paint to the foam. Firmly press the stamp onto the leggings along the seam.
4. If necessary, adjust the leggings. Continue stamping along the side.
5. Repeat on the other side. Let dry.

## STAMP OF APPROVAL

*Adding a graphic design along the seam will create an eye-catching pattern from top to bottom.*

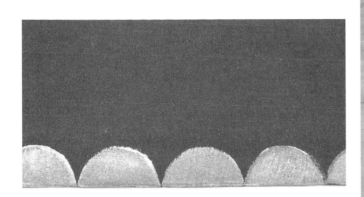

### CURVE COUTURE

*Create a scalloped pattern by cutting out a half circle instead of a triangle.*

### BACK AND FORTH

*Use two different-sized stamps for a subtle yet interesting variation.*

# Contrast-Trim Blazer

In fashion, blazers are timeless and classic pieces that will never go out of style. With a little bit of fabric glue and trim, you can add an extra something to your standard blazer.

Difficulty Level

## SUPPLIES

———

Blazer

Fabric Scissors

Small Paintbrush

Fabric Glue

Ribbon

———

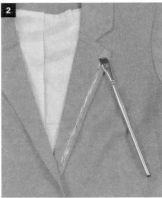

### TIP

Popping up the collar will help you glue the ribbon with ease.

1. Cut pieces of ribbon the same length as each edge of the lapel. For each piece, allow an extra 1 in (2.5 cm) at each end.
2. With the brush, thinly apply fabric glue along the edge of the lapel.
3. Lay the ribbon on top of the glue, and press lightly.
4. Continue with the remaining edges of the collar.
5. Fold the ends of the ribbons underneath the lapel, adding a small amount of fabric glue to keep in place. Let dry.

## QUITE THE CONTRAST

*Pair a bright blazer with dark ribbon for a vivid effect.*

## STYLISHLY STUDDED

*For an edgier take on the original project, outline the lapel with studs.*

### A SEQUIN LINING

*For a bit of glamour, apply sequin trim with fabric glue.*

### HEART OF GOLD

*Use a foam brush to apply metallic fabric paint all over the lapels.*

### PRINTS CHARMING

*Take a break from solid colors and use patterned ribbon.*

### ALTERNATIVE BORDERS

*Bias tape/binding is another material that can be used in lieu of ribbon.*

# Party Skirt

Plain jersey skirts are like the white canvases of DIY fashion. With such an endless variety of ribbons and trimmings available, you can make a skirt for practically every occasion. Your personalized combination will result in a fun and fashionable piece that is all your own.

Difficulty Level

## SUPPLIES

---

Jersey Tube Skirt
Stretch Sequin Trim
Fabric Glue
Scissors
Liquid Seam Sealant

---

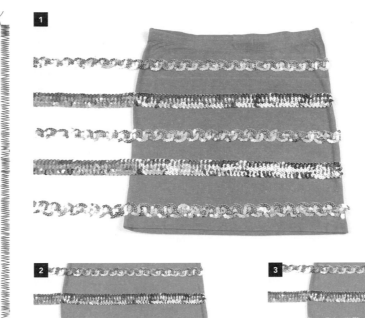

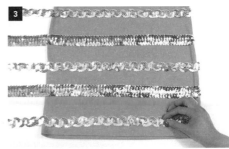

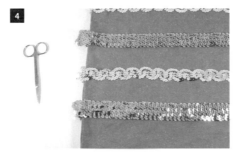

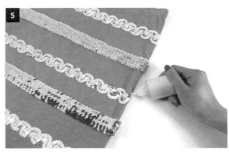

 TIP

Depending on the type
of trim, a few stitches
can be used to join the
ends together.

1. Measure pieces of trim and ribbon
   that are twice the width of the
   skirt, adding an extra 2 in (5 cm)
   to both ends.
2. Add a thin line of fabric glue
   across the skirt.
3. Place the trim on the glue, and
   press lightly. Repeat with the
   remaining trims.
4. Repeat on the reverse side and
   trim the excess, leaving just enough
   to connect to the front side.
5. Apply liquid seam sealant and/or
   fabric glue to the ends.

## WITH ALL THE TRIMMINGS

*Bring in different textures by adding stretchy braided trim.*

BALANCE OUT YOUR LOOK
BY WEARING A SIMPLE TOP
AND MINIMAL JEWELRY.
YOUR STATEMENT OF A SKIRT
WILL DO THE REST FOR YOU.

### TEXTURED TRIMS

*Glitter ribbon and
iron-on studs can add
eye-catching elements
to the mix.*

### TOP TO BOTTOM

*Switch things up by
gluing the sequin trim
in vertical rows.*

# Scarf-Panel Denim Vest/Waistcoat

Equal parts edgy and sweet, this project showcases the stunning prints found in vintage scarves. This is also a great tutorial to try out if you're just learning how to sew.

Difficulty Level

## BEFORE YOU START

To turn a jacket into
a vest/waistcoat,
cut off the sleeves along
the shoulder seam.

## SUPPLIES

---

**Denim Jacket**

**Large Vintage Scarf**

**Fabric Scissors**

**Needle and Thread
or Sewing Machine**

**Pins**

---

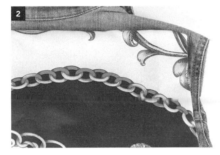 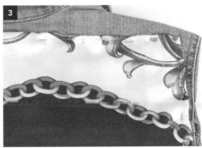

1. Trim down the scarf to fit the jacket's back panel, adding at least 1 in (2.5 cm) on each side.
2. Fold each side underneath, leaving a clean edge.
3. Pin the scarf in place.
4. Sew along each side.

## UPCYCLED STRIPES

*Salvage an old printed jersey T-shirt instead of a vintage scarf.*

## SIDEWAYS STYLE

*Purposely add an offbeat touch by cutting the scarf to one side of the central print.*

**MIX IT UP**

*Combine different types of denim by sewing leftover strips together. Leave the edges unhemmed for a distressed, frayed look.*

# Faux-Studded Leather Jacket

When it comes to outerwear, leather jackets will always steal the spotlight. You can easily "stud" your favorite number—without pliers or screws—using inexpensive acrylic buttons.

## SUPPLIES

———

**Leather Jacket**
**Button Shank Remover**
**Shank Buttons**
**Strong Craft Glue**

———

1 Remove the button shanks with the shank remover.
2 Determine the button arrangement.
3 Glue to the lapel. Repeat on the other side.

## MIX AND MATCH

*Cut the sleeves off a leather jacket. Replace with sleeves from a denim jacket by machine or hand-sewing.*

## EMBELLISHED LAPELS

*To help your "studs" blend in flawlessly, look for buttons that have the same finish as your jacket's hardware.*

## VICE VERSA

*Take the sleeves from a leather jacket and sew them to a denim vest/waistcoat.*

## WINTRY GLAMOUR

*Create an extra-chic version by adding faux fur trim to the collar and sleeves.*

## ALL THAT GLITTERS

*Accent with glitter ribbon along the pockets.*

**MAKE A STATEMENT**

*Studded trim along the shoulders adds a subtle yet fierce touch.*

# Fabric-Corner Shorts

Instead of tossing out those leftover fabric scraps, use them to dress up an old pair of denim shorts. Feel free to experiment with a variety of fabrics and to combine different textures.

**Difficulty Level**

## SUPPLIES

———

Denim Shorts

Fabric

Fabric Scissors

Pins

Needle and Thread

———

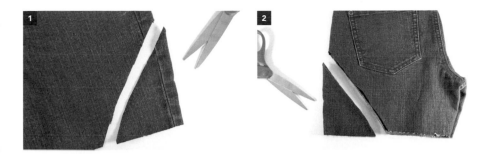

1. On one leg, cut off the outer bottom corner.
2. Fold the shorts in half. Using the first leg as a guide, cut off the corner of the second leg.
3. Unfold the denim pieces and place them on top of the fabric.
4. Cut the fabric, allowing 1 in (2.5 cm) around each piece.
5. Pin the fabric where the original corners were. Sew together with a straight stitch.

## PATTERNED REMNANTS

*Printed fabrics can instantly incorporate color into your outfit.*

## A TOUCH OF PLAID

*Vintage button-down shirts can offer interesting plaid prints.*

## FANCY FLORALS

*Add a touch of granny chic with tapestry fabric.*

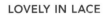

## LOVELY IN LACE

*For a more dainty combination, opt for lace.*

## OPPOSITES ATTRACT

*Use scraps from a different pair of jeans for a contrasting denim combination.*

# Gathered Dress

By adding fabric to the bottom of a tank top or shirt, you can give it another shot in your wardrobe. Wear a belt right where the two fabrics meet in order to create a slightly gathered look.

Difficulty Level

## BEFORE YOU START

Fold the fabric in half horizontally. Find the line where tank top at the hits your waist, and trim the fabric to that width plus an extra 2 in (5 cm) on each side. This will result in one large fabric rectangle that can wrap entirely around your waist.

## SUPPLIES

Loose-Fitting Tank Top

At least 1 Yard (90 cm) Fabric

Needle and Thread

or Sewing Machine

Pins

Fabric Scissors

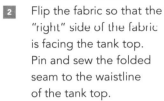

1. Fold over the top edge of the fabric ½ in (1.5 cm), twice. Pin and sew.

2. Flip the fabric so that the "right" side of the fabric is facing the tank top. Pin and sew the folded seam to the waistline of the tank top.

3. Bring the fabric back down so that the "right" side is facing up. Cut the bottom to your desired length, adding 2 in (5 cm).

4. Turn the dress inside out. Along the side, cut off the excess fabric, leaving 2 in (5 cm) beyond the intended side seam. Pin and sew to close up the dress.

5. To finish off the raw edges of the extra fabric along the side, fold it ½ in (1.5 cm), twice. Pin and sew. Repeat along the bottom edge.

EXPERIMENT WITH DIFFERENT
TOP AND BOTTOM COMBINATIONS
TO MAKE A DRESS FOR ALMOST
ANY OCCASION.

## POSH PRINTS

*Adding silk to a casual
tank top can give it a
more formal vibe.*

## DRESS UP A DRESS

*Expand your possibilities
by using an old dress
instead of a top. In this
version, black silk was
added to a pink dress for
a color-blocked look.*

# Watercolor Jeans

When it comes to fabric, dye can open up so many possibilities. The technique used in this project is extremely simple, but can yield an artsy mix of colors like blending watercolors on paper.

Difficulty Level

## BEFORE YOU START

Head outside to work on this project – it's a messy one! Protect your jeans from the ground by placing them on top of a large garbage/rubbish bag.

Some dyes require specific fabric preparation prior to using. Check the dye's packaging for any special instructions.

## SUPPLIES

---

**White Denim Jeans**

**3 Liquid Fabric Dyes (Concentrated)**

**Rubber Gloves**

**Plastic Spoon**

**Access to Washing Machine**

**Large Garbage/Rubbish Bag**

---

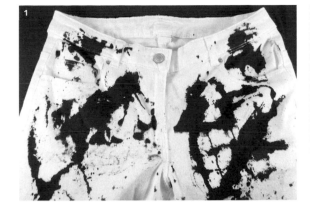

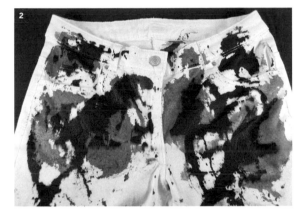

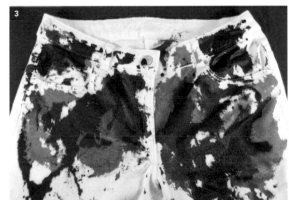

**TIP**

Powdered dyes will allow you to control the vibrancy of each color. To prepare a concentrated dye, have a heavy hand when adding the powder to water.

1. Using the spoon, and wearing rubber gloves, randomly pour the first color onto the jeans.
2. Add the second color. Don't be afraid to layer colors on top of each other.
3. Add the third color. Wait at least 30 minutes to let the dye sink in.
4. Rinse under running water until it turns clear. Toss in the washing machine—alone—for one cycle.

## BLEND THE RULES

*Leave some white areas untouched to let the dye travel. However, don't think <u>too</u> much about where you add each color—the more random, the better!*

## SUBTLE DYES

*If you prefer less vibrant colors, use a non-white garment in gray, tan, or beige. Adding more water to concentrated dye will also lighten the shade.*

## TOP IT OFF

*Use a white cotton cardigan as an alternative to jeans.*

# ACCESSORIES

From scarves to bags, accessories are some of the most useful pieces in fashion. Projects such as the Knotted Headband (page 84) can keep your hair in place, while the Sweater Circle Scarf (page 80) will keep you warm and cozy. The majority of accessory projects require just a handful of supplies, and don't hesitate to play around with new and different materials.

Accessories may take up a smaller portion of your closet, but they can accentuate your style just as much as clothing. Try thinking outside the box when it comes to specific accessories. For example, if you're a bag kind of girl, consider using various types—totes, clutches, or cross body satchels—for your next DIY. After all, there's nothing better than a project that is both functional and fashionable.

# Sunglass-Case Clutch

Small enough to fit in your hand and large enough to hold your essentials, a sunglass case can effortlessly double as a clutch. Used as a substitute purse, it can even hold your favorite pair of shades.

Difficulty Level

## SUPPLIES

Large Hard Sunglass Case
Wire Cutters
Strong Craft Glue
Stud Earring

1  With the wire cutters, remove the backing of the earring.

2  Glue the earring onto the case.

## BEJEWELED

*An earring that has lost its mate is the perfect candidate for this project.*

### A GIRL'S BEST FRIEND

*Adorn with adhesive crystals and rhinestones typically used in scrapbooking.*

### TAKE A BOW

*Make a customized bow with the same method found in the Ribbon Bow Flats (page 152).*

### HIDDEN GEMS

*Ordinary materials such as vinyl tape and be used to create stripes A vintage brooch can be repurposed as a unique embellishment.*

### RITZY RECYCLING

*Re-use metal trimmings from old clothing.*

# Elastic Brad Belt

Metal brads (also known as studs or split pins) are normally used in scrapbooking, but can easily double up as fashion embellishments. This accessory project proves that they can decorate more than just paper and photographs.

Difficulty Level

## SUPPLIES

---

Wide Stretch Elastic

Scissors

Large Metal Scrapbook Brads

Cinch Belt Buckle

Needle and Thread

Chalk Pencil

Strong Craft Glue

---

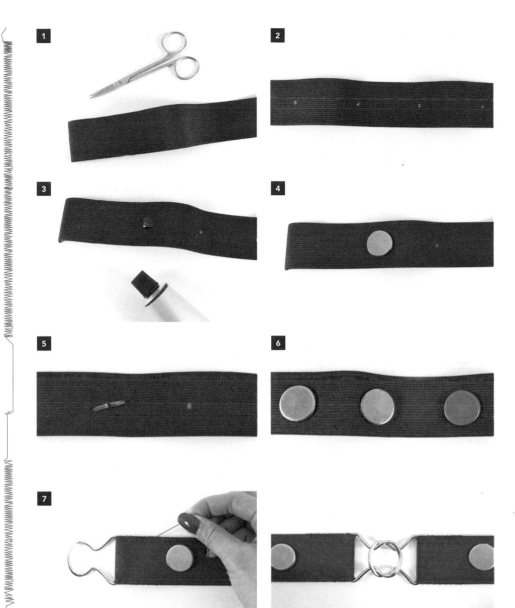

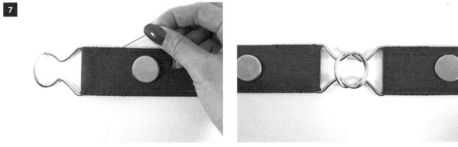

1. Cut a strand of elastic to fit around your waist, adding 4 in (10 cm).
2. Using the chalk pencil, mark dots at even intervals along the elastic.
3. Add a bit of glue around one of the dots.
4. Pierce a brad through the elastic.
5. On the reverse side, bend back the prongs to secure. You can cover the prongs with tape if you want to wear the belt over delicate fabric.
6. Repeat steps 3–5 along the elastic.
7. At one end, fold ½ in (1.5 cm) around the buckle and add a few stitches. Repeat at the opposite end.

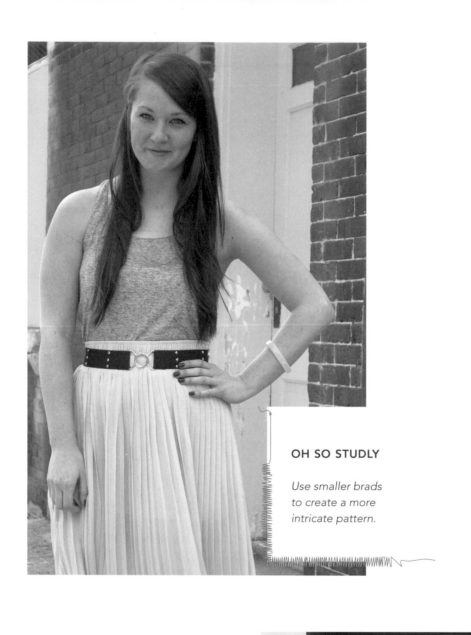

## OH SO STUDLY

*Use smaller brads to create a more intricate pattern.*

## METAL DETAILS

*When used in fashion, scrapbooking brads can give off the same vibe as studs.*

*Instead of brads, use vintage stud earrings. Remove the backings with wire cutters and glue to the elastic.*

# Stone-Strap Watch

By creating your own watch, you can tell time with style. Chunky stone beads will always make a statement, while elastic string will make your creation easily adjustable.

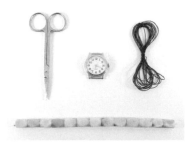

## BEFORE YOU START

Prior to purchasing a watch face at the craft store, check out any old watches you might own. A watch can be repurposed by simply cutting off the straps.

## SUPPLIES

———

**Watch Face**
**Elastic Cord**
**Stone Beads**
**Scissors**

———

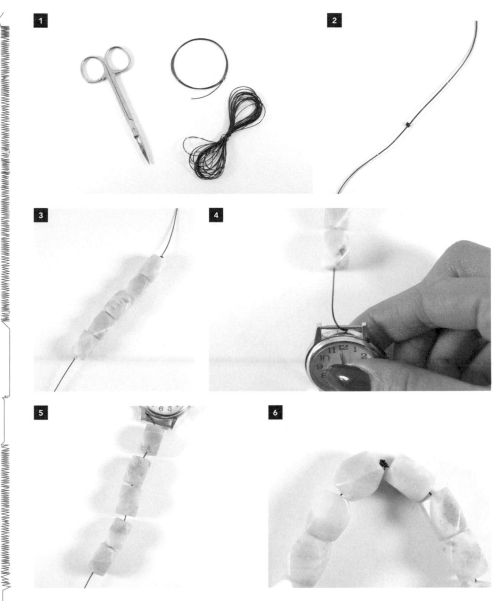

1. Cut a piece of elastic one and a half times the width of your wrist.
2. Tie a triple knot at one end.
3. String on the beads for the first half of the strap.
4. Insert the cord over and into the first loop of the watch face, under the watch and out through the second loop.
5. Add the remaining beads.
6. Tie the ends together and trim the excess cord.

## ON THE ROCKS

A watch strap made from dyed stones is ideal for wearing your favorite color in a different way.

## A NEW YORK MINUTE

Add some glamour with rhinestone connectors.

## SCRAPPY HOUR

*The same stretch fabric used for the Hardware Bracelet (page 120) can make a quick and easy watch strap.*

## A STITCH IN TIME

*Adapt the Chain-and-Thread Bracelet (page 132). Cut the chain in half before starting, and attach to the watch face with jump rings.*

## AROUND THE CLOCK

*For a rugged, chic look, use large irregular metal beads.*

# Glitter Sunglasses

The worlds of fashion and beauty go hand in hand, making nail polish an excellent DIY material. With this quick and easy project, you can wear your favorite nail polish in more than one way.

## BEFORE YOU START

Wipe excess polish off
the brush before applying
to the sunglasses.

## SUPPLIES

————

**Sunglasses**

**Glitter Nail Polish**

————

1  Apply glitter nail polish to the frames. Let dry.
2  *Optional: Clean up the frames with a cotton
swab/bud dipped in nail polish remover.*

## SPARKLING SHADES

For this project,
opt for fine glitter
nail polishes.

## SUCH A STUD

Remove the shanks
from shank buttons to
create instant stud-like
embellishments.

## SECRET GARDEN

Add clusters of
adhesive scrapbook
flowers to the frames.

## PRIM AND POLISHED

*Cut up nail polish strips and stick them onto the frames. Seal with clear nail polish.*

## LACED UP

*Floral nail decals placed directly on the lens will create the impression of a lace pattern.*

# Abstract Tote Bag

There's something about the simplicity of a canvas tote that makes it an accessory must-have. With the endless array of paint shades out there, you can add a vibrant design in your favorite color combinations.

Difficulty Level

## SUPPLIES

Canvas Tote Bag

Old Magazine or Cardboard

Masking Tape

2 Fabric Paints

Foam Brush

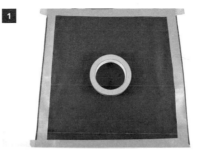

### TIP

Move the foam brush over and away from the tape, instead of toward and into it. The paint will be less likely to sneak underneath the tape this way.

1. Stick masking tape along the perimeter of the tote bag.
2. Insert the cardboard into the tote. This will prevent paint from seeping through.
3. Randomly add strips of tape.
4. Paint the first color with the foam brush.
5. Add the second color. Let dry completely.
6. Carefully peel off the tape.

*Optional: Touch up with a thin paintbrush.*

## COLORFUL GEOMETRICS

*Metallics and mattes can create a striking combination.*

## BRIGHT IDEAS

*For a more vibrant variation, use three or four colors.*

THE SIMPLEST CHANGE CAN
MAKE THE BIGGEST IMPACT.
CHANGE THE PLACEMENT OF
THE TAPE FOR A VARIETY
OF OUTCOMES.

**MULTICOLORED ANGLES**

*Slanted rows of tape will create diagonal stripes.*

**LINED UP**

*Make a striped version by placing the tape in horizontal rows.*

# Sweater Circle Scarf

Scarves might be nothing more than a long strip of fabric, but it goes without saying that they are some of the most useful accessories out there. This recycling project will keep you stylishly warm during the cooler months.

Difficulty Level

## BEFORE YOU START

About 3 or 4 sweaters should be enough to yield 10 panels. You may need more or less depending on the size of each sweater.

## SUPPLIES

---

**10 Sweater Fabric Panels**
**(9 x 19 in/23 x 48 cm each)**

**Fabric Scissors**

**Pins**

**Needle and Thread**
**or Sewing Machine**

---

1. Pin 2 panels together along their longer edges, front sides facing each other.
2. Pin a third panel to one from the first pair. Continue pinning the remaining panels in the same way.
3. Sew along each row of pins to make a long strip of fabric.
4. Fold the whole strip lengthwise, insides facing out, and pin together to make a tube of fabric. Sew along the pins.
5. Turn right side out.
6. At both ends, fold in ½ in (1.5 cm). Pin and sew.
7. Sew the ends together.

## COZY COLORS

This scarf can add color blocking to your outfit in just a second.

## CHILLY AND CHIC

A scarf made of jersey T-shirts and flannel is a prime accessory for late summer/early fall.

## SUN DAZE

*Lace and chiffon
are ideal for a
lightweight version.*

# Knotted Headband

This tutorial is an example of how one detail can completely change a project. The carefully placed knot creates the illusion that a scarf is tied around your head, when it's actually just a basic headband.

Difficulty Level

## SUPPLIES

Scrap Fabric
(7½ x 22 in/19 x 56 cm)
Wide Headband
Fabric Scissors
Needle and Thread

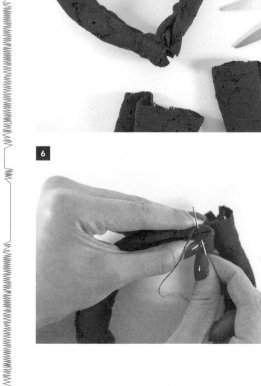

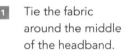

1. Tie the fabric around the middle of the headband.
2. On both sides of the knot, spread out the fabric.
3. Wrap the fabric around the headband.
4. Along the inside, sew the fabric together.
5. Trim the fabric, allowing ½ in (1.5 cm) extra.
6. Fold up and secure with a few stitches. Trim excess fabric as needed.

## STYLISHLY SAVING

*Repurpose the remnants in your stash with this hair accessory project.*

*Left to Right, Clockwise: Vintage Silk Scarf, Velvet, Bandanna, Stretch Lace*

*Left to Right,
Clockwise:
Sweater, Printed
Tights, Plaid Shirt,
Striped T-shirt*

## KNOTTY AND NICE

*You can tie the fabric
knot off to the side, or
in the middle—it's up
to you.*

# Painted Floral Clutch

Adapted from a decorating technique used on baked goods, this DIY proves that inspiration can be found absolutely everywhere. Brush embroidery, which is typically used on cookies and cakes, is a method that uses royal icing and a brush to create beautiful textured elements. With the same idea, paint can create a similar effect.

Difficulty Level

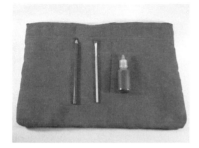

## BEFORE YOU START

Practice on fabric
or paper before taking on
the real thing.

## SUPPLIES

_____

Rectangle Clutch

Charcoal or Chalk Pencil

Thin Paintbrush

Dimensional Fabric Paint

_____

**TIP**

Squeeze some paint onto
scrap fabric to get a steady
flow before applying to
the clutch. If not, you'll most
likely start out by pushing
out air—followed by an
unwanted glob of paint!

1  With the pencil, sketch
   simple 5-petal flowers.
2  Outline with paint.
3  With the brush, drag the
   paint toward the center.
4  Paint 4 smaller petals.
5  Repeat step 3, dragging
   the paint inwards.
   Add dots of paint to
   the center.
6  Repeat until the entire
   clutch is covered.

## PLAY FLEUR KEEPS

*Don't worry about making the flowers perfect. The irregularity of each one will only emphasize the artsy, delicate look.*

## COLORFUL COMPLIMENTS

*Layer contrasting paints for a twist on the main project.*

## CENTER OF ATTENTION

*To add an extra dimension, stitch or glue an embellishment to the middle of each flower.*

### A PURSEFUL OF OPTIONS

*This painting technique works well on any type of handbag with a flat surface.*

# Embellished Beanie

Beanies can add an edgy touch to your look, but you can take it a step further and add metal embellishments in the form of metal coat buttons. To find the perfect basic beanie, check out the men's section of a clothing store around the fall and winter seasons.

Difficulty Level

## SUPPLIES

Beanie

3 Coat Buttons

Paint Pen or Marker

Needle and Thread

1. Mark dots at equal intervals with the pen.
2. Hand-stitch on the first button.
3. Repeat with the remaining buttons.

## THIRD TIME'S THE CHARM

*Coat buttons typically feature intricate designs and can add an interesting element to your headwear.*

## JUST A LITTLE BIT

*Hand-stitch a short length of curb chain for a dash of edginess.*

## A VINTAGE VIBE

*A dainty cameo flatback is ideal for adding some femininity.*

## CRYSTAL DETAILS

*Using fabric glue, top off your beanie with a pattern of faceted gems.*

# JEWELRY

When it comes to an outfit, jewelry is like the icing on the cake. It's that finishing touch that can transform a look from one occasion to the next. A basic white T-shirt is a key example; simple chain necklaces will keep it casual, while gems and rhinestones can dress it up. A statement piece such as the Beaded Circle Necklace (page 126) can complete an ensemble all by itself. Your jewelry can not only tie together your outfit, but will also give you another outlet of expression.

If you're just beginning to delve into DIY, jewelry is the perfect place to start. Since these projects tend to be smaller in size, you can experiment with various techniques and materials. Once you get a hang of basic jewelry-making skills, you'll be well on your way to spicing up your wardrobe.

# Vinyl Tube Bracelet

This project is inspired by the glitter tube bracelets that children often make in art class or summer camp. Bring in some delicate beads and vinyl tubing from the hardware store, and you'll be well on your way to creating a grown-up, chic version.

## SUPPLIES

————

Clear PVC Vinyl Tubing, Thin
(¼ in/7.5 mm in diameter)
Clear PVC Vinyl Tubing, Wide
(⅜ in/1 cm in diameter)
Masking Tape
Micro Seed Beads
Scissors
Ribbon (1 in/2.5 cm wide
and at least 14 in/36 cm long)

————

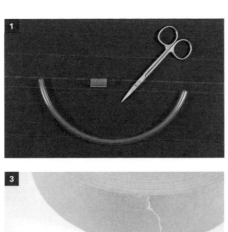

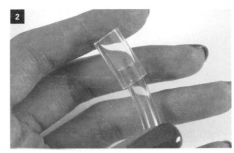

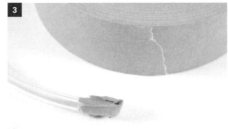

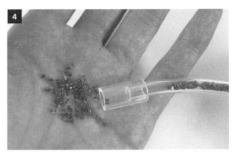

**TIP**

Hold the beads in the palm of your hand and "scoop" the beads into the tubing.

1. Cut a length of the thin tubing that is slightly longer than your wrist measurement. Cut a ¾ in (2 cm) piece of the wide tubing.
2. Attach the smaller piece to one end of the thin tubing.
3. Tape off the opposite end.
4. Carefully insert beads into the tube.
5. Continue until the entire tube is filled.
6. To close up the bracelet, remove the tape and join the opposite end into the smaller tube.
7. Tie a bow around the join and trim the excess ribbon.
   For extra security, add a dab of glue inside the bow's center.

## GOLDEN GIRL

*Metal beads can create the illusion of gold flakes.*

## CRYSTAL CLEAR

*Iridescent multi-faceted crystal beads will show off various colors when the light hits them.*

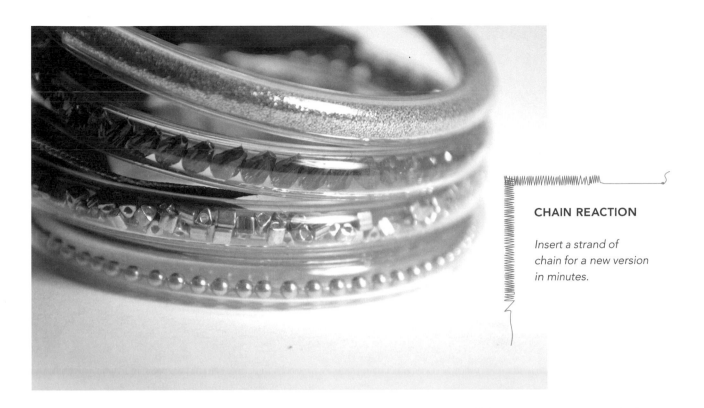

## CHAIN REACTION

*Insert a strand of chain for a new version in minutes.*

## SPARKLE CITY

*Use extra-fine glitter for a sparkling, classy alternative.*

# Triangle Drop Earrings

Just like many other basic shapes, triangular details will always be a fashion classic.
The open center of these earrings adds a hint of delicacy, while the spike charms brings
in that extra something.

Difficulty Level

## SUPPLIES

___

3-in-1 Jewelry Pliers

Tiny Metal Beads

6 Eye Pins (2 in/5 cm)

2 Jump Rings (6 mm)

4 Jump Rings (4 mm)

2 Earring Hooks

2 Metal Spike Charms

___

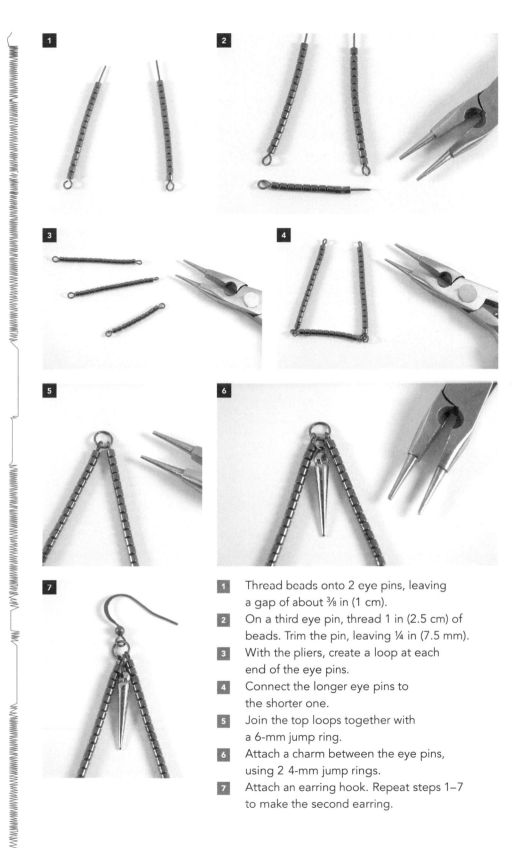

1. Thread beads onto 2 eye pins, leaving a gap of about ⅜ in (1 cm).
2. On a third eye pin, thread 1 in (2.5 cm) of beads. Trim the pin, leaving ¼ in (7.5 mm).
3. With the pliers, create a loop at each end of the eye pins.
4. Connect the longer eye pins to the shorter one.
5. Join the top loops together with a 6-mm jump ring.
6. Attach a charm between the eye pins, using 2 4-mm jump rings.
7. Attach an earring hook. Repeat steps 1–7 to make the second earring.

**METAL LININGS**

*The classic triangle shape can be dressed up or down.*

**TRUE BLUE**

*Seed beads are available in a wide variety of finishes and colors.*

## BEADED OPPOSITES

*Delicate multi-faceted crystal beads can offset the spikes in an interesting way.*

## DANGLING LINKS

*Add leftover strands of chain for a shower of style.*

# Statement Ring

Anything can happen when it comes to a ring blank. With a little glue and a creative mind, you can make practically anything into a new piece of jewelry. This project is perfect for that single earring that lost its other half.

## SUPPLIES

---

**Stud Earring**

**Wire Cutters**

**Super Glue**

**Ring Blank**

---

**1**

**2**

**1** Using the wire cutters, remove the earring post.

**2** Glue the earring to the ring blank. Let dry overnight.

**DECORATE YOUR FINGERS
WITH ODDS AND ENDS
FROM YOUR SUPPLY STASH.**

*Left to Right:
Button, Stud Earring,
Mosaic Tile, Vintage
Brooch*

*Left to Right:
Stone Pendant, Iron-On
Appliqué, Flat Bead,
Metal Pendant*

## A DASH OF ELEGANCE

*Repurpose old jewelry and components to create a one-of-a-kind cocktail ring.*

# Fabric-Wrapped Bangle

When a pair of tights has had its run, save it from the trash by wrapping it around a metal bangle. Wear it alone as a statement piece, or style it with coordinating bracelets for a wrist full of arm candy.

Difficulty Level

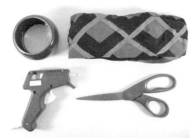

## SUPPLIES

———

Metal Bangle

Pair of Tights

Hot Glue Gun

Fabric Scissors

———

**1**

**2**

**3**

**1** Cut the tights into long strips, measuring about 1 in (2.5 cm) wide.

**2** Hot-glue a strip to the bangle, and tightly wrap around.

**3** Hot-glue the end to secure.

FROM OLD T-SHIRTS TO VINTAGE SKIRTS, CLOTHING CAN PROVIDE AN ENDLESS VARIETY OF FABRICS TO WORK WITH. DON'T BE AFRAID TO GET CREATIVE!

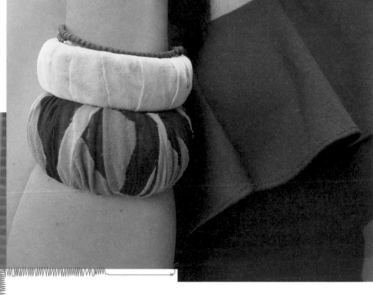

## A WRISTFUL OF STYLE

*Complement your bracelet by pairing it with a second one from the same color family, but in a different material.*

*Left to Right, Clockwise: Suede, T-Shirt Jersey, Vintage Scarf, Flannel Button-Down Shirt*

*Left to Right, Clockwise: Metallic Spandex, Printed Cotton, Chiffon, Tights*

## GRAPHIC GIRL

*Wear bold prints with a classic basic—such as a denim dress—for a look that is stylishly timeless.*

# Leather Charm Earrings

When it comes to DIY, even the smallest scraps can be transformed into a new project. This one uses metal charms in a unique way, and gives an interesting spin to conventional jewelry making.

Difficulty Level

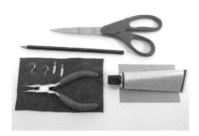

## SUPPLIES

Leather Scraps

Fabric Scissors

Cardboard

Pencil

Super Glue

Metal Charms

2 Earring Hooks

3-in-1 Jewelry Pliers

1. Cut a cardboard shape of your choice.
2. On the reverse side of the leather, trace around the cardboard shape twice.
3. Cut out both pieces.
4. Glue the charms to the tops of the leather pieces.
5. Attach the earring hooks to the charms with jewelry pliers.

### TIP

Depending on your the shape of your charm, you may need a jump ring to connect it elegantly to the earring hook.

## SUCH A CHARMER

*Flat metal charms work best for this project. Once you bring in the leather, you're essentially creating one large pendant.*

## BRIGHT LIGHTS

*Experiment with dyed leather in a vibrant color.*

## JEWEL DROPS

*Add a little glamour with flat-back gems.*

## STUDDED SCRAPS

*Iron-on studs are lightweight and easy to use. Use glue instead of heat to apply.*

## A CHARMED LIFE

*Accent with metal photo corners.*

# Hardware Bracelet

When it comes to incorporating metal elements into your jewelry, look no further than the hardware store. Odds and ends can be found at budget-friendly prices, often in a variety of sizes and finishes.

## SUPPLIES

Stretch Fabric
Fabric Scissors
Metal Pipe Coupling
Tin Can

**1**

**2**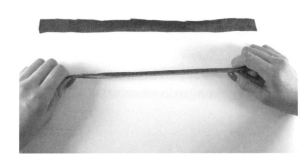

**3**

**4**

**5**

**1** Cut the fabric into two 12 in (30 cm) strands.

**2** Tug the fabric so that the edges roll up.

**3** Insert both strands through the pipe coupling.

**4** Wrap the fabric around the can. Bring both ends back around and insert through the coupling.

**5** Tie a tight double knot, and trim the excess. Slide the coupling over the knot.

### TIP

Couplings are used to join tubes and pipes together. When you're at the hardware store, scope out the plumbing section for a coupling that is similar to the one used in this project.

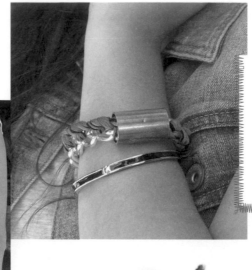

### DOUBLE TROUBLE

*Add a pipe coupling to a finished Chain-and-Thread Bracelet (page 132) for two projects in one.*

### COLORFUL COMBINATIONS

*Use scraps from different-colored jersey T-shirts.*

## SIMPLE CITY

*For a chic statement piece, use a strand of chunky metal chain.*

## HEAVY METAL

*Insert miscellaneous chains through a coupling and connect with jump rings and a clasp.*

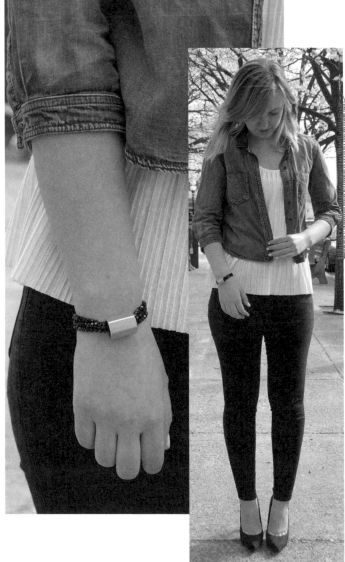

## MULTIPLE STRANDS

*Thread smaller beads onto a long strand of elastic. Insert through the coupling several times to create a multi-stranded version.*

## EDGY AND ELEGANT

*String a coupling onto a strand of elastic cord and add large faceted beads.*

# Beaded Circle Necklace

The beauty of DIY is the ability to turn an everyday object into something special. Ordinary items such as key rings can be spruced up with some beads, wire, and innovation.

## BEFORE YOU START

For each key ring, cut
a strand of wire measuring
15 times the diameter
of the ring.

## SUPPLIES

———

6 Key Rings
(1 large, 2 medium, 2 small)
2 Strands of Chain
(About 7 in/18 cm)
Package of 6/0 E/Seed Beads
3-in-1 Jewelry Pliers
8 Jump Rings (10 mm)
Jewelry Clasp
24-Gauge/0.5 mm Wire

———

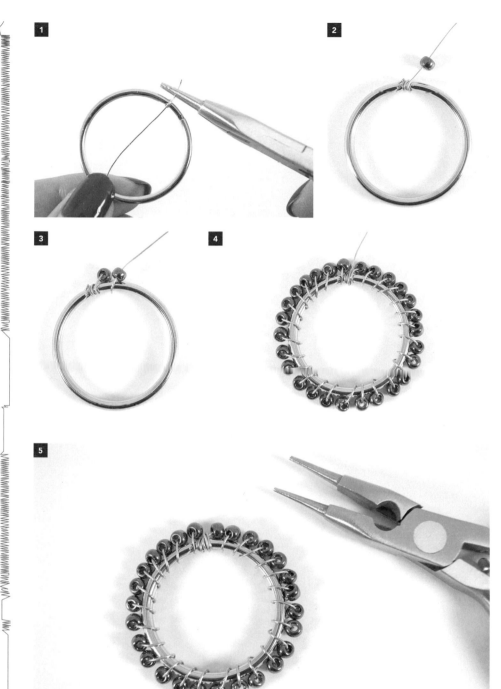

**1** Using the pliers, wrap one end of the wire tightly around the ring three times.
**2** Add the first bead.
**3** Wrap the wire around the ring and add the next bead.
**4** Continue until the ring is covered.
**5** Tightly wrap around 2–3 times, and trim the excess with wire cutters.

⊕ Continued on the next page

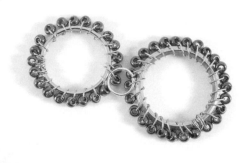

6  Repeat Steps 1–6 with the remaining rings.

7  Connect them by attaching jump rings to the wire behind the beads.

8  Using the pliers, attach a jump ring to each strand of chain.
   Attach a jewelry clasp.

9  Attach the chain to the outer key rings.

## RING LEADER

*Beads and wire can transform key rings into a stunning jewelry piece.*

## ARM CANDY

*Use shorter strands
of chain for a
bracelet variation.*

**A BEAD-WRAPPED KEY RING IS A PRIME EXAMPLE OF HOW AN EVERYDAY OBJECT CAN HOLD CREATIVE POTENTIAL.**

### SOLITARY STYLE

*Create a pendant with a single large key ring. Experiment with beads in various shapes and styles.*

# Chain-and-Thread Bracelet

Mixed-media jewelry allows you to combine diverse materials in the same project. For this bracelet, weaving thread through chain will create an interesting effect with different textures and elements.

Difficulty Level

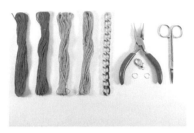

## BEFORE YOU START

Cut a strand of chain long enough to fit around your wrist.

## SUPPLIES

—

**4 Skeins of Embroidery Thread
(2 Each of 2 Colors)**

**Chunky Curb Chain**

**3-in-1 Jewelry Pliers**

**2 Jump Rings (10 mm)**

**Jewelry Clasps**

**Scissors**

—

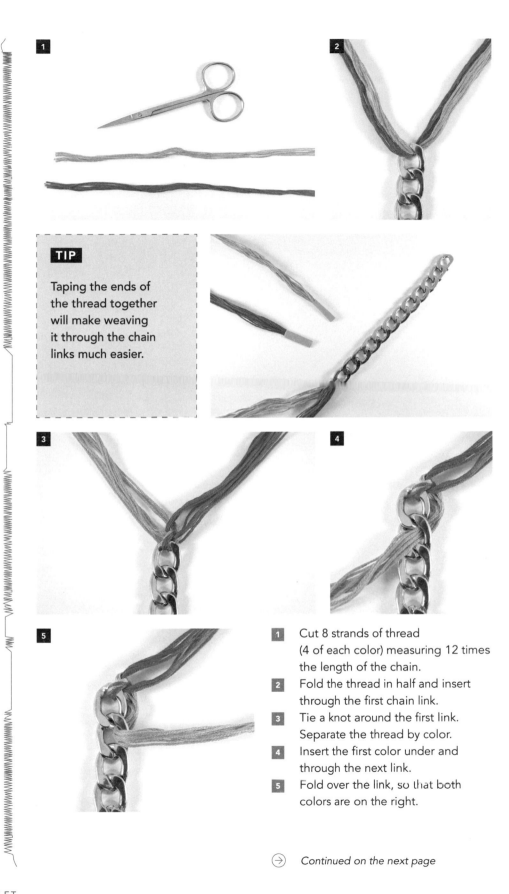

**TIP**

Taping the ends of the thread together will make weaving it through the chain links much easier.

1 Cut 8 strands of thread (4 of each color) measuring 12 times the length of the chain.

2 Fold the thread in half and insert through the first chain link.

3 Tie a knot around the first link. Separate the thread by color.

4 Insert the first color under and through the next link.

5 Fold over the link, so that both colors are on the right.

⊙ Continued on the next page

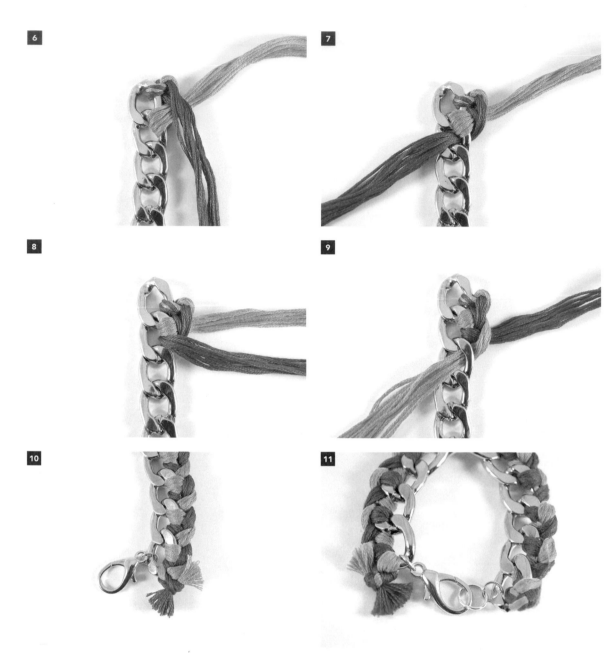

6    Place the second color over the first.

7    Insert under and through the same link.

8    Bring the second color to the right.

9    Bring the first color on top, then under and through the next link.

10    Repeat steps 5–9 down the chain until you reach the end. Tie a double knot and trim off the excess thread.

11    Using the pliers, add a jump ring and clasp.

## LITTLE MISS SUNSHINE

*A bracelet made with brightly colored thread is a great way to spruce up a casual outfit.*

## TRIPLE THREAT

*Skip step 3 and combine all of the colors together.*

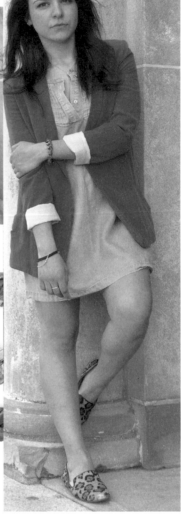

## KEEP IT SIMPLE

*Instead of multiple colors, just use one.*

## SILK VARIATION

*Replace the embroidery thread with thin ribbon.*

CHAIN-AND-THREAD BRACELET

# SHOES

For many, finding the perfect pair of shoes can be quite a task. A proper fit is one thing, while a specific style is a whole other ordeal. Different brands's sizes may run too big or small, depending on the shoe type. Luckily, DIY shoe projects allow you to use a pair that you know will fit just the way you like. The best part is that you're likely to spend just a fraction of the cost of similar pair of store-bought shoes. With some embellishments and paint, creating a personalized pair of your ideal heels, boots, or flats has never been so easy—or inexpensive!

# Studded-Sole Shoes

Metal details can give footwear an off-beat vibe that will never fall short of fashionable. Luckily, studding your own shoes is only a trip away from the hardware store. Furniture nails, which are normally used in upholstery, will give your shoes that extra kick.

## SUPPLIES

————

**Oxford Shoes (or Boots)
with Rubber Soles
Hammer
Gel Pen
Furniture Nails**

————

**1** Use the pen to make dots along the soles at even intervals.

**2** Carefully insert a furniture nail into the first dot by lightly tapping it in with the hammer.

**3** Continue around the sole of each shoe.

## SOLE SISTER

*Any shoe that has a rubber heel can be used for this project.*

## SPARKLE AND SHINE

*Glue a small rhinestone to each nail for extra glamour.*

## HIGH CLASS

*For a dressier version, use rubber-soled wedges.*

# Color-Blocked Pumps

Whether you're styling an outfit or making a project, color blocking is a great way to create a bold and classic look. With a plain-Jane pair of pumps, a little paint can go a long way.

Difficulty Level

## SUPPLIES

―――

High-heeled Platform Pumps
Masking Tape
Paintbrush
Acrylic Paint

―――

**TIP**

For best results,
use a clean,
soft bristled brush.

1   Tape off the bottom portion of the heels with masking tape.
2   Apply the paint to the heels and platform soles. Let dry in between layers.
3   Remove the tape. Repeat on the second shoe.

**CLICK YOUR HEELS**

*Painting shoes is a great way to hide any scuffs from natural wear and tear.*

**TIPS AND TOES**

*Shift the color blocking to the heels and tips for a different take on the main tutorial.*

**THE BOTTOM LINE**

*Paint stripes by using masking tape as a guide.*

**SNEAK PEAK**

*Use paint and tape on the underside for peek-a-boo stripes.*

# Floral Heels

Florals are a fashion staple that never goes out of style. Fake flowers like those used in floral arrangements can easily double as DIY materials, letting you create a springtime vibe on a budget.

Difficulty Level

## SUPPLIES

Strappy Heels
Small Faux Flowers
Wire Cutters
Strong Craft Glue

1. With wire cutters, cut off the stem and remove the plastic components, leaving just the flowers.
2. Glue the first layer of petals.
3. Add the remaining petals.
4. Glue the remaining flowers and let dry. Repeat on the second heel.

FROM ROSES TO POPPIES, YOU CAN CREATE YOUR VERY OWN WEARABLE BOUQUET.

**TICKLED PINK**

*Instead of multiple small flowers, make a statement with a single large one.*

**STRIKE A POSEY**

*The vibrant pink flowers can pull together a black-and-white outfit.*

## FLOWER GIRL

*If faux flowers are too flashy for your liking, tone it down with floral ribbon.*

# Ribbon-Bow Flats

One of the most versatile materials in your stash, ribbon makes embellishing your shoes extremely simple. This is yet another project that will help you put those miscellaneous scraps to good use.

Difficulty Level

## SUPPLIES

---

**Flats**
**Wide Ribbon**
**Fabric Scissors**
**Strong Craft Glue**

---

1

2

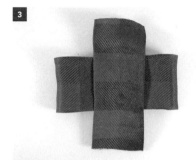

3

4

5

1. Cut two strands of ribbon measuring 7 in (18 cm) and 3.5 in (9 cm).
2. Take the longer piece and glue the ends to the middle. Let dry.
3. Fold the smaller piece around the center.
4. Turn over and glue the ribbon in place. Let dry.
5. Glue the bow to the flat. Repeat on the second shoe.

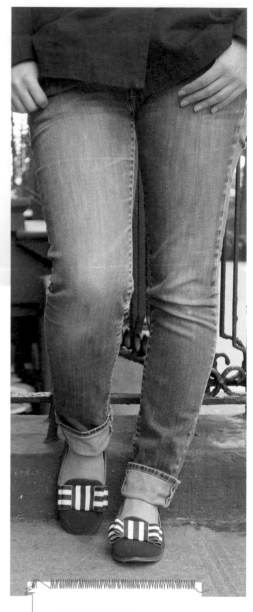

### PLAID PATTERNS

*Ribbon is useful when you are looking for new ways to add a favorite print to your wardrobe.*

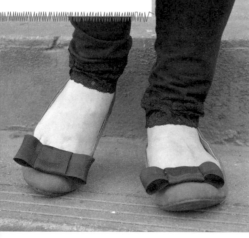

### DOUBLE TAKE

*Create layers by adding a second bow that's slightly smaller than the first one.*

## LEATHER ACCENTS

*Change things up by using leather ribbon.*

# SOURCES

## US

### GENERAL CRAFTING

Amazon.com
Ebay.com
Etsy.com
HobbyLobby.com
JoAnn.com
Michaels.com
Save-On-Crafts.com
Target.com

### SEWING AND FABRIC SUPPLIES

Fabric.com
MoodFabrics.com
MJtrim.com

### ART SUPPLIES AND SCRAPBOOKING

Dickblick.com

### HARDWARE

HomeDepot.com
Lowes.com

### JEWELRY SUPPLIES AND EMBELLISHMENTS

Rings-things.com
StudsandSpikes.com

## UK

### GENERAL CRAFTING

Amazon.co.uk
Craftsuperstore.co.uk
Ebay.co.uk
Hobbycraft.co.uk
Internationalcraft.com
Qtag.com

### SEWING AND FABRIC SUPPLIES

Josyrose.com
Love-craft.co.uk
Ribbonmoon.co.uk
Sewandso.co.uk
Vvrouleaux.com

### ART SUPPLIES AND SCRAPBOOKING

Londongraphics.co.uk

### HARDWARE

Diy.com
Screwfix.com

### JEWELRY SUPPLIES AND EMBELLISHMENTS

Beadworks.co.uk
Studsandpunks.co.uk

# GLOSSARY

**ACRYLIC PAINT**
Fast-drying paint that is suitable for a variety of surfaces. When dry, acrylic paint is water-resistant.

**APPLIQUÉ**
In fashion, a fabric or embroidered piece that is used to decorate another surface. Often has a special backing that melts and adheres to fabric when ironed. Appliqués can also be sewn or glued.

**BIAS TAPE/BINDING**
Thin strip of fabric that has been folded and pressed. Often used to finish off raw edges.

**CHAIN LINK**
"Building block" of chain. Multiple links are connected together to form a strand of chain.

**CURB CHAIN**
Chain made up of links that are slightly curved in shape.

**DRESS FORM DUMMY**
Adjustable mannequin designed to resemble a human's figure. Commonly used in dressmaking and garment adjustments.

**E-BEADS**
4 mm beads, usually made of glass. May be referred to as large seed beads, often labeled "6/0."

**ELASTIC STRING**
Stretchy, flexible cord. Available in a variety of thicknesses.

**EMBELLISHMENTS**
Small objects used for decorating fashion items.

**EMBROIDERY THREAD**
Cotton thread with six strands that can be separated, often packaged in skeins. Also known as embroidery floss.

**EYE PINS**
Straight wire pin with a loop at one end, which can be opened and closed with pliers.

**FABRIC GLUE**
Adhesive used for attaching embellishments to fabric surfaces. After 24 hours, fabric glue is flexible and machine washable.

**FABRIC MEDIUM**
Liquid that can be mixed with acrylic paint to create fabric paint.

**FLAT-BACK**
Any embellishment that has a flat surface, which can be then be glued to other items.

**GAUGE**
In jewelry making, the number used to state the thickness of craft wire. The lower the gauge, the thicker the wire; the higher the gauge, the thinner the wire.

**HEAD PIN**
Straight metal wire with a flat component at one end, which prevents beads from sliding off.

**JUMP RING**
Metal ring that opens and closes, used to join jewelry components together.

**LAPEL**
Folded collar of a blazer or jacket.

**NOTIONS**
Objects used for decorative or functional purposes, such as zippers/zips, buttons, embellishments, ribbons, and trimmings.

**PIN**
Used to keep fabric and hems in place prior to sewing.

**REMNANT**
Leftover end of a material, usually a small amount.

**RIBBON**
Narrow strip of fabric used for decorating and tying.

**RING BLANK**
Metal adjustable ring with a flat surface. Components such as buttons or embellishments can be glued to this surface.

**SEAM**
In sewing, the line of stitches that holds two fabrics together.

**SEED BEADS**
Tiny beads, usually made from glass, often used in detailed beading.

**SKEIN**
Loosely wrapped or coiled length of thread.

**SPOOL**
Plastic or wooden cylinder used to store thread or wire.

**STRETCH ELASTIC**
Flexible and stretchy strip of material that is commonly used in waistbands.

**TRIMMING**
A length of material used as a decoration or ornament, such as ribbon or fringe.

# ACKNOWLEDGMENTS

To my mother, for all the craft store trips during my childhood. Thanks for dealing with my crazy DIY projects while growing up, along with the runaway beads that were constantly found around the house. Sorry about that, but thank you for everything.

To Laurence King Publishing, thank you for making this happen. It has been an amazing experience, you are a unique publisher and I couldn't have asked for a more awesome experience while working with you. Helen Rochester, thank you so much for believing in me since the day we first met. I'm so appreciative of your guidance and patience from the very beginning. Felicity Awdry, for your input and help as I brushed up on my photography skills. Susie May and Lesley Henderson, thank you times infinity for the understanding and encouragement during the ups and downs of this eventful process. I can't even begin to express my gratitude. Sara Goldsmith, for always being so thorough, reassuring, and supportive as I learned about the world of publishing. Evelin Kasikov, for designing this book in a way that really helped me express my creativity. Though I have yet to visit, London will always have a special place in my heart thanks to Laurence King.

To the beautiful ladies who modeled in this book: Samantha Applebaum, Nicole Calascibetta, Daryl Carr, Christina Corsello, Lívia Glosiková, Rhiannon Goodman, Jessica Henning, Elena Melekos, Katerina Melekos, Dana Menusan, Amanda Mustafic, Abby Olson, Bethany Rubin, Brianna Sovak. I'm eternally grateful that each of you played a part in this journey of mine. Thank you for the laughs, the memories, and especially your time. I hope none of you have nightmares about my camera's timer going off.

This page wouldn't be complete without an extra special thank you to the stunning cover model, Lívia. Not only did your photography insight make it possible, but I'm so glad that we were able to pull together an awesome last minute shoot.

To my amazing friends, thank you for everything: Chelsea Mapa, one of my bests since we were just a few years old.

Katerina Melekos, for keeping my head on straight when I needed it the most. Dana Menusan, for your unwavering support through so much. Amanda Mustafic, for lending your creative eye during the photo shoots … "Think of the hedgehogs!"… Mackenzie Gelina, one of few people who understands my insane DIY ideas. We'll be awesome crafty cat ladies one day, in our embellished chevron rocking chairs. Rhiannon Goodman and Abby Olson, two wonderful ladies that I'm so glad to have met in college. I love how our creative minds mesh together. Here's to many more craft nights!

To my second family in Asbury Park, New Jersey – thank you for being the most supportive group of friends a girl could ask for: Erin Bermingham, Jimmy Boyce, John Cannon, Nicole Calascibetta, Howie Cohen, Jessica Henning, Erik Lindstrom, Zachary West, Garrett Yaeger, Karl Yaeger. I love you chids to pieces.

Thank you to the following people for the constant words of encouragement throughout the years: Danielle Bonsignore, Caitlin Heuberger Garrison, Sarah Mossa, Novella Nicholson, Ryan Palumbo. To those that I have worked with in some way—Milton DePaul, Nikki Fowler/*Glitter* Magazine, Blerona Kaja—thank you for the past opportunities. So much thanks to my friends all over New York and New Jersey, and my family across the United States, Canada, and the Philippines.

To M&J Trimming in Manhattan, for allowing me to take a few photos in your amazing store for the "Tips and Tricks" page. Thank you for being so supportive during all of my creative endeavors over the years. Special thanks to Dana Kamerman for absolutely everything!

To everyone who just wants to do what they love: remember that every little thing counts, even if it doesn't seem like it at the moment. As long as you're doing something, that's really all that matters. You might not know exactly where you're going—but at least you're going somewhere. Practice your passion for the sake of making yourself happy.

To every single person who has read Studs & Pearls—the blog, the book, or both—thank you. I owe you a hug.

# ABOUT THE AUTHOR

**KIRSTEN NUNEZ** is the creator of the DIY fashion blog Studs & Pearls (studs-and-pearls.com). Since launching the blog in 2010, she has been featured on CNN.com, Shine Yahoo! and MSN.com. Kirsten's work has received coverage in publications around the world, including the United States, Europe, and Australia. Outside the DIY industry, she attended college in upstate New York, where she received a bachelor's degree in Dietetics and master's degree in Nutrition. Kirsten was born and raised in New York, where she currently lives.

# INDEX OF PROJECTS BY DIFFICULTY LEVEL

No-Sew Scarf Vest/
Waistcoat
**20**

Sunglass-Case Clutch
**60**

Glitter Sunglasses
**72**

Embellished Beanie
**94**

Statement Ring
**108**

Fabric-Wrapped Bangle
**112**

Floral Heels
**148**

Party Skirt
**32**

Faux-Studded Leather
Jacket
**40**

Stone-Strap Watch
**68**

Hardware Bracelet
**120**

Studded-Sole Shoes
**140**

Color-Blocked Pumps
**144**

Ribbon-Bow Flats
**152**

Stamped Leggings
**24**

Contrast-Trim Blazer
**28**

Scarf-Panel Denim Vest/
Waistcoat
**36**

Watercolor Jeans
**54**

Abstract Tote Bag
**76**

Knotted Headband
**84**

Vinyl Tube Bracelet
**100**

Leather Charm Earrings
**116**

Fabric-Corner Shorts
**46**

Elastic Brad Belt
**64**

Triangle Drop Earrings
**104**

Gathered Dress
**50**

Sweater Circle Scarf
**80**

Painted Floral Clutch
**88**

Beaded Circle Necklace
**126**

Chain-and-Thread
Bracelet
**132**